Ways Matter CHANGES

by Thea Feldman

PEARSON
Scott Foresman

Physical Changes Of Matter

The physical properties of matter include size, shape, color, position, and mass. Physical properties can usually be changed without changing the matter. A **physical change** takes place when matter changes the way it looks without becoming a new kind of matter.

Suppose you have several pieces of wood. If you take that wood and build a birdhouse with it, you have created a new shape. What happens if you paint the birdhouse green? You have changed the color. When you put the birdhouse outside, you have changed its position.

Pieces of wood

A lot of physical changes have been made to the pieces of wood. But guess what? You have not changed the original matter of the wood. It is still made of the same solid matter. It has just been rearranged and painted, and it had its position changed.

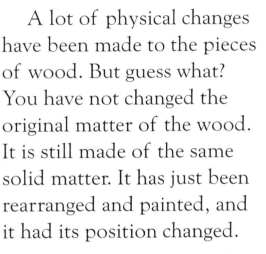

The finished, painted birdhouse outside

Different Forms
Of Matter

There are three different forms or **states of matter.** Something can be a solid, a liquid, or a gas.

A rock, a piece of wood, a drinking glass, and a kite are examples of solids. Every solid has its own mass, shape, and size.

Milk, juice, water, soup, and oil are liquids. Liquids also have mass and size. They take the shape of the container they are held in.

Most gases are invisible. You may not even realize they are there. Like liquids, gases have mass. But gases do not have size or shape.

Gases are all around you. The air is filled with gases, such as oxygen, which is an odorless and colorless gas.

Sometimes a physical change can cause the state of matter to change. But even a change in the state of matter does not change the actual matter.

When water freezes, it changes from a liquid state to a solid state. However, it is still water, just a different form of it.

A liquid, such as juice, can change into a frozen state. But it is still made up of the same matter.

Solids can change into liquids, but they are still the same kind of matter.

Matter does not change when a solid turns into a liquid either. Think about a solid block of chocolate. If you heat the chocolate, it will begin to melt into a liquid. But the particles in the chocolate have not changed. The chocolate has not turned into something else. It is still chocolate in either form.

If you let the melted chocolate cool, it will return to its original solid state. It will most likely be a different shape, so it will have undergone another physical change. But it should still taste like chocolate.

Combining Matter

Another way to change matter is to combine it with other matter. A **mixture** is two or more kinds of matter put together. The kinds of matter do not need to be put together in equal parts. A container full of nuts and bolts is a mixture. It is easy to pick out and separate the nuts and bolts from this mixture.

The most important thing about a mixture is that the kinds of matter do not change into other substances when mixed together. A mixture of pencils, markers, and crayons can easily be separated into three piles. These writing tools do not change into something else when they are mixed.

Have you ever had a mug of hot chocolate on a cold day? Do you know how it is made? Put a spoonful of instant hot chocolate powder in a mug. Then have an adult add some boiling water. What happens? The hot chocolate dissolves in the water. The water becomes a different color. You cannot see any instant hot chocolate. What you have made is a solution.

Instant hot chocolate

A **solution** is a mixture in which one or more substances dissolve into another. The hot chocolate is still in the mug. If all the liquid evaporated, you would be left with hot chocolate powder. Just like a mixture, it is usually possible to separate all the substances from a solution. Even though substances have combined, they have not really changed. Combining these substances is another example of a physical change.

Chemical Changes To Matter

Sometimes changes produce a new kind of matter. What could cause this? You know a physical change does not create new matter. During a chemical change, one kind of matter changes into a different kind of matter. Once a material has undergone a chemical change, it usually cannot be changed back to its original form.

Burning matter is one example of a chemical change. Think about a candle. First the wax melts. It changes from a solid to a liquid. This is a physical change. Then it burns. This is a chemical change. The candle has changed into gases. It cannot change back into wax again. It is no longer the same substance. It has changed chemically.

Making cookies

Baking is an easy way to see and understand how chemical changes affect matter.

If you follow a cookie recipe correctly, you will mix together flour, milk, eggs, sugar, and other ingredients to form a batter. When you bake the batter in an oven, a chemical change takes place. The batter turns into cookies. You cannot separate the ingredients from the cookies.

Baked cookies

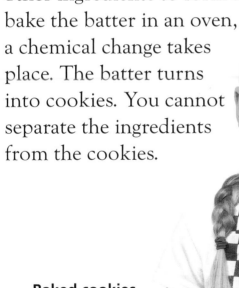

13

Chemical changes to matter can make your life better. Useful chemical changes are created by burning certain kinds of matter. Burning a candle gives you light. Burning heating oil warms your house. Burning gasoline allows your family car to run.

Baking cookies gives you something to eat. The cookies and other food you eat go through chemical changes in your body.

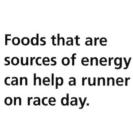

Foods that are sources of energy can help a runner on race day.

Your body breaks food down chemically into nutrients and other things you need to be healthy. Runners often eat a big meal of pasta the night before a big race. They know that food changes chemically in their bodies. Food such as pasta changes chemically into a source of energy that can help a runner on race day.

Glossary

chemical change   when one kind of matter changes into another kind of matter

mixture   a combination of two or more kinds of matter that keep their properties

physical change   when the size, shape, color, weight, or position of matter is changed

solution   a mixture in which one or more substances dissolves into another

states of matter   the different forms that matter can take: liquid, solid, or gas

What did you learn?

1. What are the three states of matter?

2. What are some examples of physical changes that matter can go through?

3. How do you create a mixture?

4. **Writing** in Science In this book you have read about how burning matter affects its state. Write to explain what happens to a candle when it is burned, using details from the book.

5. **Cause and Effect** What is the effect of mixing hot chocolate powder with hot water?

Genre	Comprehension Skill	Text Features	Science Content
Nonfiction	Cause and Effect	• Captions • Labels • Glossary	Changes in Matter

Scott Foresman Science 3.11

ISBN 0-328-13839-8

90000

9 780328 138395

scottforesman.com

Science Vocabulary Readers

Not AR

The Planets

Jeff Bauer

SCHOLASTIC